Tulsi Chalisa

Published in Sanskriti Press
Rupa Publications India Pvt. Ltd 2025
7/16, Ansari Road, Daryaganj
New Delhi 110002

Sales centres:
Bengaluru Chennai
Hyderabad Jaipur Kathmandu
Kolkata Mumbai Prayagraj

Copyright © Rupa Publications India Pvt. Ltd 2025

All rights reserved.
No part of this publication may be reproduced, transmitted,
or stored in a retrieval system, in any form or by any means,
electronic, mechanical, photocopying, recording or otherwise,
without the prior permission of the publisher.

P-ISBN: 978-93-7003-329-0
E-ISBN: 978-93-7003-821-9

First impression 2025

10 9 8 7 6 5 4 3 2 1

Printed in India

This book is sold subject to the condition that it shall not, by way of
trade or otherwise, be lent, resold, hired out, or otherwise circulated,
without the publisher's prior consent, in any form of binding or
cover other than that in which it is published.

Contents

Introduction / 5

Chalisa / 9

आरती श्री तुलसी जी की / 97

Aarti Shri Tulsi Ji Ki / 97

Introduction

The Tulsi Chalisa is a cherished devotional hymn dedicated to the sacred Tulsi plant, a symbol of purity, devotion, and spiritual blessings. Composed in reverence for this divine plant, the Chalisa extols the virtues of Tulsi, which, in Hindu belief, embodies the essence of devotion and the gateway to divine grace. The Tulsi plant, regarded as the earthly manifestation of the goddess Lakshmi, holds a place of profound reverence in Hindu homes and temples. Through its verses, the Tulsi Chalisa connects the devotee to Lord Vishnu, invoking the blessings of both material and spiritual prosperity.

Structured in forty verses, each verse of the Tulsi Chalisa highlights different aspects of the plant's divine nature, emphasizing its role in purifying the soul and fostering a sense of spiritual peace. The lyrics vividly portray the significance of Tulsi, from its spiritual qualities to its healing powers, offering prayers for well-being, prosperity, and protection from evil forces. As with many devotional hymns, the verses create an intimate connection between the devotee and the divine, encouraging deep reverence and devotion.

The tone of the Tulsi Chalisa is one of deep adoration and spiritual reverence. It flows with a gentle, meditative rhythm that invites the devotee to reflect upon the sacred nature of Tulsi and its role in the life of a devotee. Recited with love and devotion, the Tulsi Chalisa is believed to bring peace, harmony, and divine favor, transforming the lives of those who seek its blessings. Whether chanted as part of a ritual or in the solitude of personal prayer, the Tulsi Chalisa serves as a spiritual guide, offering solace, spiritual connection, and divine protection to all who recite it. Through its verses, Tulsi is not just a plant, but a symbol of devotion, healing, and eternal blessings.

Chalisa

।। चौपाई ।।

जय जय तुलसी भगवती सत्यवती सुखदानी ।
नमो नमो हरि प्रेयसी श्री वृन्दा गुन खानी ।।
श्री हरि शीश बिरजिनी, देहु अमर वर अम्ब ।
जनहित हे वृन्दावनी अब न करहु विलम्ब ।।

*Jai jai Tulsī Bhagavatī
Satyavatī Sukhadānī,
Namo namo Hari preyasī
Śrī Vṛndā gun khānī.
Śrī Hari śīśa birajinī,
dehu amar var amb,
Janahit he Vṛndāvanī
ab na karahu vilamb.*

Hail, hail to Tulsi, the divine, the truth-bearing, the giver of happiness,
I bow, I bow to the beloved of Lord Hari, Shri Vrinda, the repository of virtues.
O Shri Hari's consort, grant me the boon of immortality,
For the welfare of all, O Vrindavani, do not delay any longer.

॥ दोहा ॥

धन्य धन्य श्री तुलसी माता ।
महिमा अगम सदा श्रुति गाता ॥

Dhanya dhanya Śrī Tulsī Mātā,
Mahimā agam sadā śruti gātā.

Blessed, blessed is Shri Tulsi Mata,
Her glory is unfathomable, always sung by the Vedas.

हरि के प्राणहु से तुम प्यारी ।
हरीहिं हेतु कीन्हो तप भारी ॥

Hari ke prāṇahu se tum pyārī,
Harīhīṁ hetu kīṇho tap bhārī.

You are dearer to Lord Hari than His very life,
For His sake, you performed great penance.

जब प्रसन्न है दर्शन दीन्ह्यो ।
तब कर जोरी विनय उस कीन्ह्यो ॥

Jab prasann hai darśan dīnhyo,
Tab kar jorī vinay us kīnhyo.

When He (Lord Hari) was pleased and gave His darshan (divine vision),
Then, with folded hands, I made my humble request.

हे भगवन्त कन्त मम होहू ।
दीन जानी जनि छाड़हु छोहु ॥

He bhagavant kanta mam hohū,
Dīn jānī jani chhāḍāhū chohū.

O Lord, make my heart Your beloved,
Knowing my helplessness, never abandon
me or forsake me.

सुनि लक्ष्मी तुलसी की बानी ।
दीन्हो श्राप कध पर आनी ॥

Sunī Lakṣmī Tulsī kī bānī,
Diṇho śrāp kadh par ānī.

Hearing the words of Lakshmi and Tulsi, She (Tulsi) was given a curse that came to pass.

उस अयोग्य वर मांगन हारी ।
होहू विटप तुम जड़ तनु धारी ।।

Us ayogya var māṅgaṇ hārī.
Hoho vitap tum jaḍ tanu dhārī.

The one who is unworthy, yet seeks a bride.
O Lord, You have assumed a form with eternal roots and support.

सुनी तुलसी हौं श्रप्यो तेहिं ठामा ।
करहु वास तुहू नीचन धामा ॥

Sunī Tulsī hiṁ śrapyo tehiṁ ṭhāmā.
Karahu vās tuhū nīcan dhāmā.

Hearing this, Tulsī (the poet) was cursed to that place.
Reside there, O Lord, in the abode of the lowly.

दियो वचन हरि तब तत्काला ।
सुनहु सुमुखी जनि होहू बिहाला ।।

Diyo vachan Hari tab tatkālā.
Sunahu sumukhī jani hohū bihālā.

The Lord gave His word at that very moment.
Listen, O auspicious one, do not be distressed.

समय पाई व्हौ रौ पाती तोरा ।
पुजिहौ आस वचन सत मोरा ॥

Samay pā'ī vhau rau pātī toṛā.
Pujihau āśa vachan sat morā.

When the time comes, I shall offer prayers
and fulfill your promise.
I will worship with hope, for my words
are truthful.

तब गोकुल मह गोप सुदामा ।
तासु भई तुलसी तू बामा ।।

Tab Gokul mah gop Sudāmā.
Tāsu bhai Tulsī tū bāmā.

Then, in Gokul, the cowherd Sudama.
Tulsī (the poet) says, you (the Lord) are
the left-handed one.

कृष्ण रास लीला के माही ।
राधे शक्यो प्रेम लखी नाही ॥

Kṛṣhṇa rāsa līlā ke māhī.
Rādhe śakyo prem lakhī nāhī.

Krishna's dance (Rasa Leela) is beyond measure,
Radha's love is so intense that it cannot be quantified.

दियो श्राप तुलसिंह तत्काला ।
नर लोकही तुम जन्महु बाला ॥

Diyo śrāp Tulsīh tatkālā.
Nara lokhī tum janmahu bālā.

The curse was given to Tulsī at that moment,
And thus, you (O Lord) were born in the human world.

यो गोप वह दानव राजा ।
शङ्ख चुड नामक शिर ताजा ॥

Yo gop vah dānav rājā.
Śaṅkha cuḍ nāmak śir tājā.

That gopa (cowherd) was once a demon king,
Shankhachud, who wore a crown made of a conch.

तुलसी भई तासु की नारी ।
परम सती गुण रूप अगारी ।।

Tulsī bhī tāsu kī nārī.
Param satī guṇ rūp agarī.

Tulsī became his wife,
A supreme chaste woman, full of virtues
and beauty.

अस द्वै कल्प बीत जब गयऊ ।
कल्प तृतीय जन्म तब भयऊ ॥

As dvai kalpa bīta jab gayau.
Kalpa trītya janma tab bhayau.

When two Yugas (cycles of time) passed and went by,
In the third Yuga, her rebirth occurred.

अवृन्दा नाम भयो तुलसी को ।
असुर जलन्धर नाम पति को ।।

Vṛndā nām bhayo Tulsī ko.
Asura Jalandhar nām pati ko.

She was named Vṛndā (Tulsī).
Her husband was the demon king
Jalandhar.

करि अति द्वन्द अतुल बलधामा ।
लीन्हा शंकर से संग्राम ॥

*Kari ati dvandv atul baladhāmā.
Līnhā Śaṅkara se saṃgrām.*

Engaging in a great struggle with immense strength,
She fought a battle with Lord Shiva.

जब निज सैन्य सहित शिव हारे ।
मरही न तब हर हरिही पुकारे ॥

Jab nij sainya sahit Śiva hāre.
Marahī na tab Har Harīhī pukāre.

When Lord Shiva, along with his army, was defeated,
He did not die and instead called out, Har Har!

पतिव्रता वृन्दा थी नारी ।
कोऊ न सके पतिहि संहारी ।।

*Pativrata Vṛndā thī nārī.
Ko'ū na sake patihi sanhārī.*

Vṛndā was a devoted wife,
None could harm her husband.

तब जलन्धर ही भेष बनाई ।
वृन्दा ढिग हरि पहुच्यो जाई ॥

Tab Jalandhar hī bheṣh banā'ī.
Vṛndā ḍhiga Hari pahuchyo jā'ī.

Then, Jalandhar disguised himself,
And Vṛndā (Tulsi) went in search of
Lord Hari.

शिव हित लही करि कपट प्रसंगा ।
कियो सतीत्व धर्म तोही भंगा ॥

Śiva hit lahī kari kapaṭ prasangā.
Kiyo satītv dharm tohi bhangā.

In the name of Lord Shiva, he engaged in deceitful actions,
Thus, breaking your chastity and virtue.

भयो जलन्धर कर संहारा ।
सुनी उर शोक उपारा ॥

Bhayo Jalandhar kar sanhārā.
Sunī ur śok upārā.

Jalandhar was slain by the Lord. Hearing this, her heart was filled with sorrow.

तिही क्षण दियो कपट हरि टारी ।
लखी वृन्दा दु:ख गिरा उचारी ॥

*Tihī kṣaṇa diyo kapaṭ Hari ṭārī.
Lakhī Vṛndā duḥkh girā ucārī.*

In that very moment, the Lord removed the deceit.
Seeing this, Vṛndā spoke words of great sorrow.

जलन्धर जस हत्यो अभीता ।
सोई रावन तस हरिही सीता ।।

Jalandhar jas hatyo abhītā.
So'ī Rāvan tas Harīhī Sītā.

Jalandhar, though powerful, was slain,
Similarly, Ravana, though mighty, was
defeated by Lord Hari and lost Sita.

अस प्रस्तर सम हृदय तुम्हारा ।
धर्म खण्डी मम पतिहि संहारा ।।

As prastara sam hriday tumhārā.
Dharm khaṇḍī mam patihi sanhārā.

Your heart is as hard as a stone,
You have destroyed my husband's dharma and life.

यही कारण लही श्राप हमारा ।
होवे तनु पाषाण तुम्हारा ॥

Yahī kāraṇ lahi śrāp hamārā.
Hove tanu pāṣāṇ tumhārā.

For this reason, you have received our curse.
May your body turn into stone.

सुनी हरि तुरतंहि वचन उचारे ।
दियो श्राप बिना विचारे ॥

*Sunī Hari turatahi vachan uchāre.
Diyo śrāp binā vichāre.*

Hearing this, Lord Hari immediately spoke,
And without consideration, He gave the curse.

लख्यो न निज करतूती पति को ।
छलन चह्यो जब पारवती को ॥

*Lakhyo na nij kartūtī pati ko.
Chalan chahyo jab Pārvatī ko.*

He did not realize his own actions towards his husband,
And desired to deceive when it came to Pārvatī.

जड़मति तुहु अस हो जड़रूपा ।
जग मह तुलसी विटप अनूपा ।।

Jaḍamati tuhu as ho jaḍarūpā.
Jag mah Tulsī viṭap anūpā.

You, being foolish, have turned into a stone-like form,
In this world, Tulsi is an unparalleled plant.

धग्व रूप हम शालिग्रामा ।
नदी गण्डकी बीच ललामा ॥

Dhagv rūp ham Śāligrāmā.
Nadī Gaṇḍakī bīch lalāmā.

We take the form of the Śāligrāma (stone).
In the midst of the Gaṇḍakī river, we shine brightly.

जो तुलसी दल हमही चढ़इहै ।
सब सुख भोगी परम पद पईहै ॥

Jo Tulsī dal hamhī caṛh ihaiṅ.
Sab sukh bhogī param pad paīhai.

Those who offer the Tulsi leaves to us here,
They will enjoy all pleasures and attain the supreme position.

बिनु तुलसी हरि जलत शरीरा ।
अतिशय उठत शीश उर पीरा ।।

*Binū Tulsī Hari jalat sharīrā.
Atiśay uṭhat śīś ur pīrā.*

Without Tulsi, Lord's body burns with fever,
Excessive pain rises in His head and heart.

जो तुलसी दल हरि शिर धारत ।
सो सहस्त्र घट अमृत डारत ॥

Jo Tulsī dal Hari shir dhārat.
So sahastr ghaṭ amṛt ḍārat.

Whoever offers a Tulsi leaf on the Lord's head,
They pour nectar from a thousand pots.

तुलसी हरि मन रंजनि हारी ।
रोग दोष दुःख भंजनी हारी ॥

Tulsī Hari man rañjanī hārī.
Rog doṣ duḥkh bhanjanī hārī.

Tulsi is the beloved of Lord Hari's heart,
She is the destroyer of diseases, faults,
and all sorrow.

प्रेम सहित हरि भजन निरन्तर ।
तुलसी राधा में नाही अन्तर ॥

Prema sahit Hari bhajan nirantar.
Tulsī Rādhā mein nāhī antara.

With love, continuous devotion to Lord Hari,
In Tulsi, there is no difference from Radha.

व्यन्जन हो छप्पनहु प्रकारा ।
बिनु तुलसी दल न हरिहि प्यारा ॥

Vyanjan ho chappanahu prakārā.
Binū Tulsī dal na Harīhi pyārā.

There are fifty-six varieties of dishes,
But without the Tulsi leaf, Lord Hari does not find them dear.

सकल तीर्थ तुलसी तरु छाही ।
लहत मुक्ति जन संशय नाही ॥

Sakal tīrth Tulsī taru chāhī.
Lahat mukti jan sanśaya nāhī.

All the holy places are found in the Tulsi tree,
Those who seek liberation find no doubt.

कवि सुन्दर इक हरि गुण गावत ।
तुलसिहि निकट सहसगुण पावत ।।

Kavi sundar ik Hari guṇa gāvat.
Tulsīhi nikat sahasaguṇa pāvat.

The poet beautifully sings the praises of Lord Hari,
And by being close to Tulsi, one gains thousands of virtues.

बसत निकट दुर्बासा धामा ।
जो प्रयास ते पूर्व ललामा ॥

Basant nikat Durbāsā dhāmā.
Jo prayās te pūrv lalāmā.

Near to it resides the abode of Durbāsā,
Where the efforts made earlier are seen to shine.

पाठ करहि जो नित नर नारी ।
होही सुख भाषहि त्रिपुरारी ॥

Pāṭh karahi jo nit nar nārī.
Hohee sukh bhāṣahi Tripurārī.

Those who read it daily, both men and women,
Will attain happiness and speak the words of Lord Tripurari (Shiva).

तुलसी चालीसा पढ़हि तुलसी तरु ग्रह धारी ।
दीपदान करि पुत्र फल पावहि बन्ध्यहु नारी ॥

सकल दुःख दरिद्र हरि हार ह्वै परम प्रसन्न ।
आशिय धन जन लड़हि ग्रह बसहि पूर्णा अन्न ॥

लाही अभिमत फल जगत मह लाही पूर्ण सब काम ।
जेई दल अर्पही तुलसी तंह सहस बसहि हरिराम ॥

तुलसी महिमा नाम लख तुलसी सुत सुखराम ।
मानस चालीस रच्यो जग महं तुलसीदास ॥

Tulsī Chālīsā paṛhī Tulsī taru graha dhārī.
Dīpādān kari putra phal pāvahi
bandhyahu nārī.

Sakal duḥkh daridr harī hār
hway param prasanna.
Āśīya dhan jan laṛahi graha
basahī pūrṇā atra.

Lāhī abhimat phal jagat
mah lāhī pūrṇa sab kām.
Jeī dal arphī Tulsī tam'h
sahas basahī Harīrām.

Tulsī mahimā nām lakh Tulsī sūt sukhārām.
Mānas Chālīsā racyo jag mahm' Tulsīdās.

Those who recite the Tulsi Chalisa, and worship the Tulsi plant,
Offer a lamp and they will gain the fruits of having children, and barren women will conceive.
All pain and poverty will be removed, and the devotee will be blessed with supreme joy.
Their house will be full of wealth, and they will live in peace, their stars aligned.
They will receive the results of their desires, and all their endeavors will be fulfilled.
Whoever offers Tulsi leaves, Lord Hari will reside in their home with a thousand blessings.
The glory of Tulsi is immense, and the name of Tulsi brings joy and peace.
The creation of the 'Manas Chalisa' by Tulsidas is renowned in the world.

आरती श्री तुलसी जी की

जय जय तुलसी माता, सबकी सुखदाता वर माता।
सब योगों के ऊपर, सब रोगों के ऊपर,
रुज से रक्षा करके भव त्राता।
जय जय तुलसी माता।

बहु पुत्री है श्यामा, सूर वल्ली है ग्राम्या,
विष्णु प्रिय जो तुमको सेवे, सो नर तर जाता।
जय जय तुलसी माता।

हरि के शीश विराजत त्रिभुवन से हो वंदित,
पतित जनों की तारिणि, तुम हो विख्याता।
जय जय तुलसी माता।

लेकर जन्म बिजन में आई दिव्य भवन में,
मानव लोक तुम्हीं से सुख सम्पत्ति पाता।
जय जय तुलसी माता।

हरि को तुम अति प्यारी श्याम वर्ण सुकुमारी,

प्रेम अजब है श्री हरि का तुम से नाता।

जय जय तुलसी माता।

Aarti Shri Tulsi Ji Ki

Jai Jai Tulasi Mata, Sabki Sukhadata Var Mata
Sab Yogo Ke Upar, Sab Rogo Ke Upar,
Ruj Se Raksha Karke Bhav Trata
Jai Jai Tulasi Mata

Bahu Putri Hai Shyama, Sur Valli Hai Gramya,
Vishnu Priya Jo Tumko Seve, So Nar Tar Jata
Jai Jai Tulasi Mata

Hari Ke Shish Virajat Tribhuvan Se Ho Vandit,
Patit Jano Ki Tarini, Tum Ho Vikhyata
Jai Jai Tulasi Mata

Lekar Janma Bijan Me Aai Divya Bhavan Me,
Manav Lok Tumhi Se Sukh Sampatti Pata
Jai Jai Tulasi Mata

Hari Ko Tum Ati Pyari Shyam Varna Sukumari,
Prem Ajab Hai Shree Hari Ka Tum Se Nata
Jai Jai Tulasi Mata

Aarti Shri Tulsi Ji Ki

Victory, victory to Tulsi Mata, the giver of happiness to all.
Above all yogas, above all diseases,
By protecting from ailments, you are the savior of the world.
Victory, victory to Tulsi Mata.

Many sons are born to Shyama, and the village is adorned by the sun,
Those who serve you, O beloved of Vishnu, they attain liberation.
Victory, victory to Tulsi Mata.

Lord Vishnu resides on your head, revered by all three worlds,
You are the redeemer of the fallen souls, widely known.
Victory, victory to Tulsi Mata.

Born in a divine mansion in the world of the gods,
It is through you that the human world attains prosperity and happiness.
Victory, victory to Tulsi Mata.

You are extremely dear to Lord Hari, the dark-skinned, tender maiden,
The love between you and Lord Hari is beyond measure.
Victory, victory to Tulsi Mata.